THE COUPLES TREASURE CHEST

The Seven Most Effective Ways to Move Your Relationship from Misery to Joy

Dr. Richard Nongard
CouplesTreasure.com

The Couples Treasure Chest:
The Seven Most Effective Ways to Move Your Relationship from Misery to Joy
by Dr. Richard K. Nongard

Copyright © 2020 by Dr. Richard K. Nongard
All Rights Reserved.

No part of this publication may be reproduced, distributed, or transmitted in any form or by any means, including photocopying, recording, or other electronic or mechanical methods, without the prior written permission from the author, except in the case of brief quotations embodied in critical reviews and certain other non-commercial uses permitted by copyright law.

The stories in this book are fictional representations of typical cases Dr. Nongard has worked with. Names, characters, places and incidents are products of the author's imagination or are used fictitiously. Any resemblance to actual events, locales, or persons living or dead is entirely coincidental.

First Printing: July 2020

ISBN-13: 978-1-7344678-2-6

Dr. Richard K. Nongard

Subliminal Science Press

15560 N. Frank L. Wright Blvd. B4-118

Scottsdale, AZ 85260

(702) 418-3332

www.RichardNongard.com | www.CouplesTreasure.com

Dr. Nongard is available to be a speaker at your event and speaks on a variety of topics.

About Dr. Richard K. Nongard:

Dr. Richard K. Nongard is a Licensed Marriage and Family Therapist, and the author of numerous books on counseling, hypnotherapy, mindfulness, and leadership. Dr. Nongard is a frequent conference and keynote speaker for community organizations, mental health groups, and businesses.

His most recent notable accomplishment was sharing his story, and how mindfulness can transform your life, at TEDx Oklahoma City in April of 2019.

Dr. Nongard has completed his Doctorate in Transformational Leadership with a concentration in Cultural Transformation through Bakke Graduate University. BGU is a nationally accredited university, accredited by an accreditor which is recognized by both the United States Department of Education (USDOE) and the Council for Higher Education Accreditation (CHEA). He holds a master's degree in counseling from Liberty University (Class of 1990).

Richard is an innovative leader in the field of psychotherapy and Mindfulness, and over the last 25+ years he has trained thousands of professionals including ministers, medical doctors, psychologists, social workers, family therapists, hypnotherapists and professional counselors in ways to do a better job serving their clients.

He is the author of many textbooks and resources. Recent titles include:

The Step-Spouse: How to Stay Sane when Their Ex is Driving you Crazy

Real-Hope: How Hope Drives Positive Actions that Lead to Business, Leadership and Real-World Victory

The Step-Spouse: What to Do When Their Ex is Making You Crazy

The Seven Most Effective Methods of Self-Hypnosis

Turn Around Trauma: How to Live Your Best Life After Adversity

You can access the free resources that accompany this book at: CouplesTreasure.com

Table of Contents

Chapter One 1
  What Happy Couples Save
Chapter Two 17
  Filling Your Treasure Chest
Chapter Three 27
  Hazards in Treasure Hunting
Chapter Four 34
  Positive Intentions
Chapter Five 44
  Positive Words
Chapter Six 54
  Positive Emotions
Chapter Seven 63
  Positive Touch
Chapter Eight 73
  Invest in Time
Chapter Nine 81
  Live in the Present
Chapter Ten 94
  Cultivate Good Relationship Habits
Chapter Eleven 102
  Cashing in Your Treasure

Dr. Richard K. Nongard

Chapter One
What Happy Couples Save

Have you ever fantasized about what it would be like to discover a treasure trove? What would you do with those riches if you found them? How far forward in your life could you go? This book is about finding a treasure—a personal, rich treasure buried deep inside your current relationship.

Each of you readers will experience this book differently. Perhaps you are the reader who knows this treasure does exist, but you have let so many difficulties pile on top of it, that you must dig hard to find it again. Or perhaps you are the reader who is uncertain of the existence of this treasure, feeling that your relationship has always been difficult and nothing can change. At this point in your life, however, you are willing to look for that treasure in case its existence is real, therefore making change possible.

When I was a kid, my grandmother collected S&H Green Stamps. These were loyalty stamps that the local grocery stores gave out to encourage ongoing shopping. They could be collected, and later redeemed for various prizes and merchandise giveaways. The more you shopped, the better your kitchen utensils. My grandmother would hoard these stamps. Her kitchen drawer was filled with long rolls of green stamps, books where she would paste them as proof of her treasure, and occasionally there were orange stamps in the drawer as well. These orange stamps were super stamps that carried the value of as many as 100 green stamps.

When my grandmother filled enough books, we would trek to the S&H Green Stamp store. It was filled with accessories for the home and kitchen. Some were priced as low as one book for redeeming, others required five or ten books. The most valuable items were set on display in the middle of the store, and in order to acquire these items, literally thousands of stamps and multiple books were needed. Every time my grandmother would cash out, we would carry the items to her Buick Electra 225 and clumsily fill the massive trunk of her massive car.

Afterward, we would go for a special treat. I suppose she was in a good mood with all of her free wares, and she would take me to get soft-serve ice cream at the Dairy Queen with the money she saved by getting free stuff from the green stamp store. This was back in the late 1960s and was a super special treat for a little kid like me.

Dr. Richard K. Nongard

Fast forward. As a licensed marriage and family therapist, I have seen that many people run their marriage the same way my grandmother did her grocery shopping. They save certain types of "marital green stamps" instead of cashing these in for amazingly awesome kitchen gadgets and products for the home (and the occasional ice cream treat for a kid with the money saved).

But there is a difference. Instead of saving the stamps for buying things at the store, they save the marital green stamps by making mental notes of every mistake, negative behavior, or self-serving attitude demonstrated by their partner. Rather than saving these in books, they save them mentally, cataloging in their memory a list of wrongs, irritations, and difficulties their partner has caused. Just like the orange stamps, which were worth a bunch of green ones, in collecting marital green stamps partners collect super stamps for behaviors and words that are particularly egregious.

Instead of cashing out the marital green stamps for fantastic prizes as my grandmother did, couples tend to save their marital green stamps for just the right moment of revenge, retribution, or anger, and use them as justifications for their negative behavior, their harsh words, and even the ultimate prize: breakup and divorce.

In a lot of relationships, it works like this: Chris noticed every time Ash didn't take out the trash as she had agreed to do. This added to Chris's feeling that Ash just didn't pay attention to the little things that were important. Every time Ash didn't take out the trash, another mental green stamp was added to the book Chris was keeping. Last month Ash had lied about being at work late, and Chris felt like an adequate explanation was not given. For Chris, this was a big deal. But to avoid further conflict, Chris just added one of the big orange stamps to the book.

A few months later, Chris and Ash had a huge fight. Emotions were high, conversation was tense. In a moment of anger, Chris cashed in those emotional green stamps and escalated the argument by justifying harsher words than usual. When Ash responded with pain, Chris dug deeper by doubling down and pulling out the green stamps, itemizing everything Ash had failed at in the past six months.

In more extreme examples, infidelity or other significant issues can fill up an entire stamp book with one single action. Joe had promised his wife, Margaret, that he would never drink to excess again. But after getting a DUI in the company vehicle and losing his job, Margaret cashed in the green stamps she had saved, justifying an affair she had encouraged with a man from her neighborhood. She moved out in a whirlwind of frustration, emptying the bank accounts and taking the kids to her mother's home in another state.

Obviously, in this example, Joe had significant behavioral issues and likely an alcohol abuse problem. It is important to understand that sometimes, ending a relationship where there is infidelity, substance abuse, emotional abuse, or other significant issues, might be the best course of action for all parties involved, including the children. But in this case, rather than address the real issues head-on, Margaret compounded the problem by saving up those stamps and justifying her own non-resourceful behavior. Both Joe and Margaret need help; saving green stamps is not the right course of action for either party.

These emotional green stamps lead to misery in a relationship. Relationships are often initially built with a promise. But unfulfilled promises, personal failure, personality disorders, and communication failure can frequently drive one or both parties in a relationship to start saving these emotional green stamps.

Rarely does a relationship begin poorly and just get worse from there. In almost every significant relationship, marriage, or other long-term relationship, things begin with high hopes, promises, and a mutual desire to succeed. First-date pictures are taken, couples brag to their friends that they have the best catch, and wedding pictures are taken as the cake is cut. For many couples, the downward spiral of relationship misery occurs slowly. To avoid open conflict, filing these emotional green stamps for later use becomes the pattern.

Sometimes, just a handful of stamps are cashed in by complaining to friends and family about the partner, or by withholding affection for a day or two. Sometimes bigger prizes of conflict are cashed in, including harsh words, distancing from the partner, or selfish behavior. At some point, though, the drawer of the emotional green stamps will be full, and then it's time to seriously cash them in. Perhaps you have seen the relationships of your friends and family? Do you notice these redeeming acts in others? What about your own relationship?

- Passive-aggressive behavior
- Withholding affection or sex
- Unkind words to your partner
- Refusing to admit wrongs until your partner admits them first
- Emotional or physical affairs
- Giving the silent treatment

- Avoidance
- Gossiping and revealing a partner's intimate details
- Procrastinating
- Undermining your partner's successes or accomplishments
- Rigidity without compromise

This, of course, is only a partial list. But if you see these behaviors in your relationship, then either you, your partner, or both of you have been saving up these emotional green stamps. The slide from initial hopes in a new relationship to battling daily misery is often a slow downward motion. People do not realize the severity of their misery as compared to the hopes they once had. It seems that for many couples, the years go by, and misery becomes the new norm, with the green stamps continually filling the drawers.

When I work with couples, both parties are usually aware of the misery, and neither are happy. Since misery loves company, part of the downward spiral is that they share their misery by tit-for-tat redeeming of the stamps they have collected. When couples come into my office, they often sit on opposite sides of the room, feeling no hope and wondering if counseling is even worth it. They wonder if reconciliation is possible, and they wonder if they can reignite the spark that brought them together in the first place.

In almost every couples session that I have done, I shared this metaphor of collecting green stamps. It resonates with people. They see how the problems started small, and by not dealing with the little things immediately, they stored up those stamps and got into the habit of redeeming them for short-term emotional satisfaction (revenge). They also saved the big ones to justify some pretty negative behaviors. In the previous example, it is pretty clear that Joe likely has a substance abuse problem that predated the relationship. However, not only did Margaret cash in her stamps by justifying her affair, but Joe also cashed in his by blaming Margaret for why he drank too much.

If you find yourself in a relationship like Chris and Ash, you can repair the emotional world and return to love and fulfillment by stopping the habit of collecting green stamps. If your relationship is about to head over the cliff of misery, with extreme behaviors such as those Joe and Margaret demonstrated, there is also hope. With serious attention to the alternatives, and a real desire to change, you can reverse the course of your misery and find joy.

Dr. Richard K. Nongard

I know it might seem impossible. The good news is that feelings are not facts. Many couples have found that by practicing proven principles of positive psychology and addressing emotions, thoughts, and behaviors in new ways, misery can transform to hope and love, just like hope and love transformed to misery at some point. As you read this book, set aside your feelings of fear, hopelessness, and misery for a short time and start implementing the proven solutions.

The ideas in this book come from my personal experiences navigating difficult relationships, as well as my work with clients in the therapy office. Furthermore, the concepts discussed come from evidence-based research into relationship psychology, as they describe the tools couples can use to restore passion and hope in their lives.

The ideas in this book will work best if you and your partner work through these techniques together. But if your partner is not interested or willing to cooperate, then here's the plus side: Each strategy I share can stand on its own. This means that even if at this point you are the only willing participant, then by simply implementing these ideas, you will notice a change. Your partner will notice these changes as well. And just like the partner who starts his own green stamp collection to compete with yours, intentionally or unintentionally, he will likely start to match or mirror your efforts and then change.

What is the alternative to collecting green stamps?

The alternative to saving emotional green stamps is to start saving relationship treasures. It's amazing how many of us are primed to note what is wrong but fail to notice what is right. This is true not only in relationships but in business and community life as well. People have a natural tendency to magnify the negative, to find fault, and identify problems. How do we redirect this negative behavior into positive action? The answer is to create new habits that force us to start living in the solution rather than the problem. What does this mean, and how does it work?

In business, a company might have an 8% customer dissatisfaction score. This might be a reflection of customer complaints, failed deliveries, faulty installations, or other similar failures. In business, almost every meeting is devoted to "knowing more about the problem" and "finding solutions to what is wrong." This is a natural inclination for almost every business and industry. The issue is that when we persist in looking at the problem, we are living in the problem and not in the solution. Some businesses have mastered a new way of looking at this age-old issue. The new process that these businesses are implanting is called Appreciative Inquiry. Case Western Reserve University has dedicated an entire program in its school of business to teaching this new method.

Appreciative Inquiry in business breaks the old pattern of meeting after meeting discussing and looking at problems, then setting them aside. Instead of looking at the 8% failure rate, they look at the 92% success rate! They have meetings that look at what they are doing correctly and what their satisfied customers appreciate. Instead of trying to do less of what is wrong, they try to do more of what is right.

Positive psychology is an academic discipline that looks at psychology differently than traditional therapy. In traditional therapy, we look at depression and anxiety or other problems and try to find solutions to the misery. Again, this stays in the problem. If in every counseling session the therapist asks how their patient's depression is today and what they notice about how their depression has changed, they are still talking about depression (or anxiety, or any other therapeutic issue). Positive psychology asks a different question. It asks, "When do you notice happiness?" and it asks, "What can we do that is happy?" Instead of reflecting on the problem, it focuses on the solution.

The Couples Treasure Chest

If you and your partner have been ruminating about your misery in the relationship and are busy saving those stamps, it is time to try something different. I give this assignment to almost every couple I work with in the first session. It is called the "Couple's Treasure Chest."

During our session, I give them a spiral notebook, the kind a high schooler would have for a class. I also give them a Sharpie pen and ask them to write "The Smith/Jones Treasure Chest" on the cover of the notebook. Then I instruct them to take the book home and put it in a room where both of them will be each day—the bedroom, kitchen, bathroom, living room, and so on.

One book. Two people.

Here are the instructions:

Each day, write down one thing you value about your partner. You can write one word. One short sentence. One short paragraph. But nothing more than that.

Do not discuss what you have written. (For many of the couples I work with, discussion will escalate things. Passive-aggressive comments like, "How come you never said that before!" can result in cashing in green stamps before this project even gets off the ground.)

Dr. Richard K. Nongard

Each day, read what your partner has written, and each day, add something new to the notebook. Anything. Something big or something small. (For some couples, this is extremely difficult.) *If it is difficult for you, try your best, and write one thing you observed, noticed, or felt. It should be phrased in a positive manner. This is the time to remember the old adage, if you can't say something nice, don't say anything at all. It does not have to be detailed, it can be short. It could even be just one word. The point is to start saving treasures rather than green stamps.*

I ask the couples I work with to bring this to each session. I read what they have written. It is amazing how one week of doing this can change the dynamic of misery to one of tolerance. The most amazing things happen when couples do this for months on end; when they do it for a year; when they fill up one book and have to start filling another treasure chest.

You can do this entire activity as well. If you do this, you will discover hidden treasures. You will discover that under the tension, behind the anger, deep behind the layers of misery are some hidden gems. There is a reason you and your partner came together, and those reasons may have been long forgotten. But, with the right tools, you can still find them under the sand and mud, just like buried treasure on an uninhabited island hideaway.

The Couples Treasure Chest

This project—creating a couple's treasure chest—is not just for couples who have high levels of misery. Couples can use this as a strategy to *prevent* misery. In any relationship, tough times will come. Learning periods will exist. It is during these times that the stored or hidden treasures can be cashed in and prevent the relationship from spiraling into misery. There is not a couple on Earth that could not benefit from this exercise. Also, it is fun to do!

The emotional green stamps are generally redeemed for justification, revenge, and power. When couples stop collecting these and start collecting treasures, they get to cash in on the treasure of some really wonderful things. Sometimes they cash in a few stamps for a pleasant evening or a night of making love. Sometimes they save the treasure and cash in a few weeks of treasure collecting for empathy or understanding or creating a shared experience.

I love it when couples I have worked with for a long time cash in the treasure for the life they have always wanted, the life they fantasized about on their first date, or at the altar when they had their first kiss.

Treasures saved result in some magnificent growth. These treasures result in helpful communication, honesty, trust, sexual faithfulness, and real emotional support. Imagine what your relationship could become if you start digging for treasure rather than saving those nasty stamps.

This book is a guide. If you implement every idea in this book, I can just about guarantee that you will find new peace and a new happiness. But implementing every idea is not necessary. I am sharing a multitude of ideas, based on the science of relationship satisfaction and the experiences of successful couples work. Even if you only implement a handful of these ideas, you will produce results.

How do you eat an elephant? One bite at a time. As you go through this book, implement the ideas. Try them out. If one idea works for you, then keep doing it. If you find it is not practical for your relationship, then move on to the next idea and try it out. Then go back and retry the more difficult ideas. Even if your partner does not engage in these ideas at first, keep trying. There is always hope. You can implement any of these ideas without your partner's support or participation.

You probably want your partner to change. And objectively, they might even need to change for the relationship to work in the long run. But change must begin with you and your own willingness. You make the change you want in this relationship. Let that be your

The Couples Treasure Chest

starting point. Your partner will come around in due time and join you in this hunt for hidden treasures.

You can access free resources that accompany this book at: CouplesTreasure.com

Dr. Richard K. Nongard

Chapter Two
Filling Your Treasure Chest

Now that you have started the treasure chest let's look for some other ways to fill it with treasure! In this book, I am going to share with you the seven ways to move from misery to joy. Some of these will be techniques you and your partner can integrate into your relationship; some will be more philosophical and are ideas you can adapt as your own. Adapting new ideas and attitudes can have practical results. In relationships, we only know what we know. Perhaps you did not have healthy relationships modeled for you, and the result has been that you have only known how to have a miserable relationship. This is the case for many of us.

To do something different, we must change both our thoughts and actions. Techniques like the treasure chest change our actions. Changing our thoughts is equally important. The good news is that with learning new things, we can adapt new beliefs, and new beliefs result in new actions. The outcome of this is a better relationship, one where we have a chest filled with treasured moments, memories, and treasured experiences.

The Couples Treasure Chest

A few years ago I was sitting in the office of my friend Carla. She and her husband Kevin own a small auto dealership. Over the years, I have purchased many cars from them. It was their 30th anniversary, and they were planning to head out to dinner. I asked Carla, "What is your secret to 30 years of happy marriage?"

Without missing a beat, she turned to me and said, "Find someone who has a set of problems you can live with, and then live with them!" That is some profound advice. Far too many couples go into a relationship with the intent or belief that the little things that bother them will change. In reality, these things rarely change, and sometimes these irritations become amplified (another source for more green stamps). The attitude of acceptance is required for long-term success in any relationship. This does not mean any behavior or problem will always be acceptable (lying, dishonesty, betrayal, criminal behavior, abuse, etc.) but that we must recognize our partner, like ourselves, has both good qualities and personal deficits. Acceptance does not mean we learn to like these things; rather, that we don't let those things engage us. We throw away the green stamp rather than saving it. The result is that 30 years later, we can look back and say, "It has been good," even if there have been challenges.

Through implementing the ideas in this book, you will be able to cultivate treasure in your relationship. Have you ever thought, "If only I could win the lottery, then my problems would all be fixed?" The reason we have this thought is that we know wealth and treasure can make a huge difference in our lives. But not all treasure comes in gold bars and silver coins. Treasure in a relationship is just as valuable as a chest full of cash. Acceptance, love, forgiveness, gratitude, and many other treasures can sustain you during difficult times and help you to enjoy the best that life has to offer.

There are seven key concepts in this book. Each of these will be explored, and I will provide you with practical ways to dig up the treasure in each category and bank it for your long-term future. The result will be amazing. Even before you are halfway through, you will begin to notice joy where there has been misery and an ability to see things differently in the present moment than you have in the past. You will no longer wish to just be happy again; you will actually activate happiness. You will no longer wish to have "what you once had" as you will have something even better—bankable treasure you can cash in at any time to make your relationship even better.

The opening line of the book asked what it would be like to discover a hidden treasure trove. Now imagine what it would be like to have a rock-solid and happy relationship without having to go through the pain of breaking up and finding a new love. Imagine what it would be like to be with your partner and experience joy rather than sadness, or support rather than loneliness. It would feel just as amazing as discovering that treasure chest, wouldn't it?

The seven most effective ways to move your relationship from misery to joy are:

1) Explore the treasure of positive intentions
2) Discover the treasure of positive words
3) Distribute the treasure of positive emotions
4) Share the treasure of positive touch
5) Cultivate mindfulness
6) Create positive and valuable time
7) Unearth positive habits

At first glance, it is obvious that these are things that might be found in a couples' treasure chest or that they would be pathways to moving a relationship from misery to joy. After all, who does not know that good communication, positive words, and pleasant emotions help people? For most people, the problem is not knowing what the treasures are. After all, most of us can envision what might be in a pirate's treasure chest: Gold doubloons, bricks of silver, rare gems, and gold jewelry.

Rather, the problem is knowing how to find the treasure and enrich our relationships as a result of these discoveries.

We have already learned one valuable lesson in how to start storing up treasure in our first chapter, and the rest of this book is going to be devoted to helping you now unpack the treasure chest and benefit from the riches in your relationship. A miserable relationship is really miserable. It is miserable not only for us but for our partner also. Couples that begin to store up treasures invest in their relationship and find that misery can move to joy in due time.

I do want to point out that as you follow the instructions in this book, the relationship wealth that you will create has a compounding rate of return. What this means is there is no technique in this book that will create overnight riches. Instead, as you begin to pack your treasure chest, its value will multiply over time. When I was a kid, I was fascinated by learning that if I saved just one penny today, two pennies tomorrow, and four pennies the next day that at the end of thirty days, I would have over five million dollars! In the real world, compounding interest pays huge rewards. If I save $1,000 a month for 40 years, the end result will be that my wealth would be over $3,000,000—yet, I would have only contributed less than 20% of that money. In real terms, the law of compounding interest means that I get to take out far more than I put in.

These economic principles are going to be at work in your relationship. The more you put in, the more you will be able to take out when you need it! Instead of free money, it is free love, free joy, and free happiness.

I want to point out the difference between happiness and joy. Both are important. Happiness is a feeling we create when something works out well or in our favor. It tends to be more fleeting and is often present when our immediate needs are met. Joy, on the other hand, is not simply a lot of happiness, or even just accepting our partner despite their faults and irritations. Joy is about internal satisfaction. Joy is about being in a state of happiness that extends to multiple situations and experiences. Joy is about driving home from work and not having to worry if there will be a fight tonight and smiling as you confidently walk in the door. Joy is about knowing that even if there is disagreement, there is resolution and that minor irritations or differences can be resolved because the relationship as a whole is moving in the right direction.

According to George Valliant, a Harvard University psychiatrist, "Joy is all about our connection to others," and what it does is create an enduring sense of wellbeing, first in our subconscious and then throughout our whole being. Joy is enduring and has the power to transform relationships and create lasting success.

Joy brings a smile to our face, it makes us feel security and significance when in the presence of our partner, and joy protects us from anxiety and fear. Without a doubt, you know many couples, some old and some young, who consistently have joy in their relationship. Perhaps you have marveled at how such a wonderful relationship is even possible or been envious of their seemingly perfect fairytale life. In reality, the fairytale does not actually exist, and if you were to see their private moments, you would probably notice some things that were simply not wonderful. Yet, joy is there? How did these couples do it? They did it by storing up relationship treasure, and they know how to live on the dividends of the wealth treasure creates so that when tough times come, they do not descend into misery.

I am going to teach you step-by-step how you can unpack these treasures and build a misery-proof relationship. But you will need to know what your intentions are. By buying this book, it is pretty clear living joyfully is your hope, and probably your intention. That is a great start. But now we must ask, "What if our partner does not want to change, and thinks it's all my fault, and only I am the one who needs to change?"

If this is your situation, I have good news for you. These seven proven methods for moving a relationship from misery to joy will work if both of you share the intentions of living joyfully and do these exercises together. But even without the participation of your partner in these techniques and methods, even if you are the only one reading this book and using the principles contained herein, they will produce change. This is a powerful reality that should fill you with hope if you are not getting the participation from your partner at this time.

In psychology, we call this principle Emotional Contagion. Just like a cold can be caught and passed from one person to the next, emotions create shared experiences as well. To this point, you have both caught the contagion of misery. This is your current experience. If both of you work towards recovery, perhaps you will move to joy together faster. But in the end, even if only one partner is willing to start "taking the medicine" of positive psychology, the result will be infectious, and most likely, your partner will eventually begin to get your symptoms. In this case, the symptoms of happiness, joy, positive intention, and the symptoms of a better relationship.

What research has shown is more amazing than the simple fact that our happiness or joy can create joy or happiness in others. Research done at Harvard by medical sociologist Nicholas Christakis shows that the happiness we infect others with can last up to a year! It can be enduring. This is how the treasure chest works. We literally store up relationship wealth and bank it so that we can access it at any time. Christakis also found that when our emotional contagion of joy infects our partner, it can then be transmitted to others, including children, in-laws, and extended networks of friends. Christakis and his research partner James Flower also found that good habits like weight loss and smoking cessation can be contagious as well. This book is filled with new habits, and just by being close to you, your partner will become infected with the positive changes that you make!

Recognize that you do not have to battle your partner to change them. I know we all want fast results and that our current culture of instant and fast access to anything and everything makes us impatient. But good things come over time, and your partner will catch your infection of joy. In cases where you are willing to make changes and

The Couples Treasure Chest

your partner is not, an old parable I learned years ago comes to mind: The stream said to the river, you go quickly, I go slowly, together we reach the sea.

Dr. Richard K. Nongard

Chapter Three
Hazards in Treasure Hunting

To this point, my message has one of hope, and I have made wonderful promises. I have promised that no matter how much misery you have accrued and how many marital green stamps you have acquired, you can stop collecting those stamps and turn your relationship around. By storing treasures in your relationship, and finding the hidden gems that have been there all along, you will find a new serenity and a new peace, and move from misery to joy.

The rest of the chapters of this book will also be filled with hope and promises, and my sincere wish is that you discover joy. But no journey to hunt treasure comes without warning. In real life, treasure hunting is filled with warnings, dangers, and things that can put an end to a treasure hunt. The hunt for real-life treasure may run up against catastrophic weather that impedes an expedition, political issues that stop either travel or the collection of treasure. Real-life treasure hunting can end in a mutiny among those seeking the treasure, and wild animals and other natural risks can also put an end to the hunt.

The Couples Treasure Chest

In Austria, Lake Toplitz was a naval base during World War II. It is believed that the Nazis sunk hidden treasure filled with gold into the lake. Over the years, hundreds have attempted to find this lost treasure, and many have lost their lives in pursuit. Sunken logs halfway between the surface of the lake and the bottom of the lake keep this treasure hidden.

In Arizona, the Lost Dutchman gold mine has mystified those who have hunted its treasure for more than 170 years. Jacob Waltz was the first to seek its fortune, a bounty left behind by a wealthy Mexican family who was killed by natives of the land. Many have hunted its treasure, but its treasure is rumored to be guarded by a curse. One man is alleged to have found the mine, a man mysteriously named Ruth. The problem is he broke his leg in the wilderness before he could bring an excavation team, and his body was found with a note saying he discovered the mine and needed help. Perhaps the curse is what did him in?

The Seychelles islands and La Réunion is rumored to be littered with hidden treasures. The most famous of these rumored treasures is 70 million dollars' worth of pirate treasure buried on one of these islands, most likely the island of Mahé. Again, many have failed because of the dangers of hunting the rugged and remote terrain for this treasure. Reginald Herbert Cruise-Wilkens dedicated the last 27 years of his life to finding this treasure, earning the nickname the "Treasure Man." The crevices and caverns of the island allegedly conceal this loot, but pathways blocked by boulders and underwater tunnels keep the treasure from being discovered. Currently, the Treasure Man's son continues the quest, but now the government has imposed a fee of 250,000 rupees to get a license to continue the search. The lesson being, if it's not one thing, it is another.

In your quest to uncover the bounty, I promised in the first two chapters of this book that I want to warn you of some obstacles along the way. In my nearly 30 years as a Licensed Marriage and Family Therapist, I worked with many people who have succeeded in turning misery into joy, but I have also met those who, on the precipice of discovering the treasure, lost it all.

These are the major hazards couples face in trying to discover treasure. There are five emotional and relational dangers that you must avoid. These are:

- Resentment (grudges)
- Jealousy
- Passive-Aggressiveness
- Selfishness
- Unrealistic Expectations

There are, of course, other things such as gaslighting in a relationship, emotional or physical abuse, addiction, and even unrequited previous love that can endanger a relationship or even tell you it is time to end the hunt and look for a different treasure. Professional treasure hunters can become quite wealthy, and some people hunt treasure for a living. These people know when it's time to give up a hunt and seek new treasures because the problems are insurmountable.

Betrayal can also sabotage the hunt, as can legal issues, complications with step-spouses and in-laws, and profound sexual or financial differences. These issues, though, are not the domain of this book. These require intervention at a professional level for fortunes to be reversed, or at least seriously good communication patterns between partners and a willingness to change. Some of these, like a broken leg in the wilderness of the hot Arizona desert, can be fatal to a relationship. I am not one to endorse staying together at all costs. I believe that when the problems are insurmountable or even dangerous, rather than losing our life in the pursuit of treasure, it is completely rational to give up the hunt in one location and look in another.

At this point, I am going to assume that you know there is treasure. The problems you have in your relationship are the nagging problems that drive two people apart and cause ships to take a different course, rather than the types of problems that put your life, or the lives of your children, at risk. This is why we are going to deal with the hazards of the Couples Treasure, because as difficult as these might seem to overcome, each one of them can be overcome.

To overcome these five hazards of making change, you must first be willing to deal with them in your own life, and you must be able to recognize them. The reason is simple. These are *your* issues, and you have the power to manage them. Often in relationships, people will say things like, "She hurt me so much, I can't just forget." Or things like, "I can't even find anything good because he makes me so angry."

Yes, in these situations, our partner probably did wrong us. But the reality is that no matter what they have done, *we* control our response. It is natural to respond to anger with anger or to hurt with hurt. Or to disappointment with depression, or betrayal with jealousy. Yet, the principle of psychological flexibility can allow us to put some space between us and our emotions and choose a response that has long-term benefits rather than short-lived expressions of anger. When we change our response, they will change their response.

One practical way to do this is to change your response time. If you have a short fuse, make the fuse longer. Do this by counting three breaths between the words that cause so much pain and your response. This is not yoga; you do not have to take three deep breaths or even slow breaths. What you are doing is practicing counting the next three breaths. On the fourth breath, you can respond. What this exercise does in situations of stress is it changes instinctual reactions to actual responses. Three breaths are enough time for the mind to catch up to the emotions. If you do nothing else in this book, do this. It can change the dynamics of a relationship.

The great thing about this exercise is that it can be done privately in your own head. The person who has stirred the pot, even intentionally, is unaware of your counting. When you provide a response rather than a reaction, the entire dynamics of the situation will change. It is perhaps one of the simplest ideas in this book, but one of the most profound.

Perhaps it seems too simple! Try it out. Even if your conversations are not tense, practice pausing and counting three breaths to even simple questions or statements. "Where would you like to go to dinner?" The instinct is to respond with "anywhere," but that is not a helpful answer to either you or your partner. To your partner, it becomes frustrating, and you might miss out on what you want because if you answer "anywhere," they might just select the place you like the least.

When you pause, count three breaths. Your brain will catch up to your impulses, and rather than blurting out "I don't care" or "anything," you will have had enough time to be assertive and name the place you actually would like to go. The result? No frustration and you get the dinner of your choice. It works every time.

Chapter Four
Positive Intentions

Intentions create our experience. The first treasure you can seek is intention. Nothing that exists in this world exists without intention. A desk does not make itself, a car does not build itself, and even an autonomous vehicle had to be programmed by someone with intention. Intention is what creates our reality, and it is for this reason that it is the foundation of a happy marriage.

Someone who set the intention to have a happy relationship is far more likely to discover happiness than someone who is a responder to circumstances and looks to see how they feel in light of current situations. Intentions must be set. You must set the intention to have a happy relationship and look for happiness to acquire it. Without setting an intention, you are going to react to your world, and reactions are rarely joyful.

Marriages can often be an example of lost intentions. In 30 years of doing therapy with clients, I have seen the following trend over and over. A young couple sets the intention to live happily ever after. And so they work together to reach their goals. The first goal is the wedding, usually followed by a starter house, and a car and a kid or a dog. A few years after reaching their initial goals, they have lost sight of their intention and are bogged down by the tasks of the day, and the immediate needs of finances, children, or business.

The couple forgets that they intended to spend time together, or intended to dream together, or even just play together, and they drift apart. The goals are still there—but the intention is not. This is the source of the seven-year itch for most couples, and unfortunately, psychotherapy is a lot like business. Rather than focusing on intention to fix it, most therapists help people set new goals on top of old goals, making the problems ultimately worse.

Have you been setting your goals, failing to reach them, and then have become frustrated with goal setting? For many people, this is the case. We rarely even advocate goal setting in relationships! When I share this with people, they often report that they have learned SMART goal setting, a particular type of goal setting that is widely advocated in corporate work, sales training, and personal improvement seminars. When we delve into the research on goal setting, though, we discover that setting SMART goals might not actually be that smart. So, what is the alternative? After all, isn't it true that if you aim for nothing, you will hit nothing?

At this point, I want to clarify the difference between goals and intentions. There is a lot of talk in the business world about goal setting, and relationship experts will give you the advice that couples need to set new goals and always be working towards something. A goal is something you want. A goal is something you are working towards. Often, a goal is set to meet the expectations of others (like a grandmother wanting a grandchild), and goals are almost always focused on the future. The problem with goal setting is that the only moment we actually have power over is this moment. Another issue is that goals set my customary expectation or others are not goals that we have set, and so there is no buy-in. Goals can also be a pathway to spiraling mediocrity, as our psychological propensity when we are not reaching our goals is to revise our goals downward. These things happen whether the goals were sales goals at work or goals in a relationship.

The alternative to goal setting is intention setting. Unlike goals, intentions don't have to wait for the future or even for change to occur. Even if you are miserable in your relationship at this moment, you can set the intention to be joyful. You might not be joyful, but the intention can be there. You might not even see how it is possible to be joyful, but yet, you can set an intention right now. You have control over this moment. In fact, it's the only moment you have control over.

Intentions begin with "I am" statements. I am joyful. I am resilient. I am a treasure finder! The great thing about "I am" statements is that nobody can say "I am" for you. We own intentions. Nobody can say, "I am," except you. Unlike goals, we have full ownership of intentions. I can intend to be happy, joyous, and free, but nobody can intend this for me.

You own your intention, unlike goals which are often assigned or set by others. What this means is that you can set an intention in your relationship right now, even if your partner does not share the intention. Unlike goals, which will always fail if partners do not work together towards the goal, intentions can be activated with or without the participation of your partner.

Intentions are very powerful because the moment you set them, you define the path you are going to follow to seek your treasures. If you look for joy, you will find joy. If you look for love, you will find love. It has been said that "where your attention goes, your energy flows," and the result of setting intentions is an immediate pathway to what is truly most important to you.

The Couples Treasure Chest

A better skill to help you find buried treasure in your relationship than goal setting is intention setting. When we develop this skill, we will look back at the periods where previously we used to set goals and realize that any goals we would have set were wildly surpassed with intention setting.

Intentions, on the other hand, are immediate. You can set the intention to be healthy right now, even if there are problems with your physical condition. We can set the intention to be wise with money, even if we don't believe we have enough. We can set the intention to be wise, even if we have made mistakes in the past. Do you see the difference? I can be healthy, wealthy, and wise right now, and by doing so, I create the likelihood that in the future, these elements will exponentially grow.

Sam and Debbie went into their marriage believing they were the perfect couple. When Sam asked Debbie to marry him, they decided to set their wedding date almost a year from the proposal. They wanted a memorable wedding, one that celebrated both families, and they sought a destination wedding on a Florida island. Sam was a sales manager and good at goal setting. Debbie was a teacher who set learning goals for students. Now they had a shared goal. As the date drew closer, they set the goal of finding the perfect house to buy after the wedding. They wanted to be homeowners within six months.

They had other shared goals, such as doubling up on student loan payments and becoming debt-free. They put $14,000 in deposits on their credit card for the wedding, and they wanted that paid off within the first year. Sam and Debbie were so good at goal setting that they planned to have their first child in year three and a second child in year six. On their seventh anniversary, they toasted to reaching all their goals while other couples they knew struggled.

By year ten, Sam and Debbie were miserable with each other. They were so good at setting goals that they missed the power of now to transform a relationship. Rather than setting the intention to be financially responsible, they set targeted financial goals. They focused on the future but missed the moment. Rather than setting the intention to be a family filled with joy, they set goals and timetables for planning their family. They often felt that they could not enjoy the present because they were working for their future.

Because Sam and Debbie reached almost every goal they set by year seven, they now were existing without new goals. Sure, they planned to buy a bigger house—a forever home—and would also need new cars; but cars, of course, only last a few years. For the past three years, they felt they were growing apart, with each one working on maintaining the success they had achieved. To any outsider, Sam and Debbie seemed to have it all. But for them, each day was one filled with responsibility and feeling like they had to be productive in order to be happy. When all the big goals were reached, they were left without purpose and felt as if they were just existing in their home.

Stories like this are not uncommon. Many couples are good at goal setting and even reaching their goals. The problem for Sam and Debbie, and other couples, is that goal setting can create security, but they also miss the power of the present. Sam and Debbie, and other couples like them, have missed out on the power of setting intentions. They never examined what they really wanted. Sure, they knew they wanted a home, but never looked at the intention behind it. The intention of homeownership might be security, or status, or even intimacy and connection. When you were shopping for a home, you probably looked for that space you could share as a couple. This is an intention. The intention of shared experience.

The mistake couples often make is to believe security, shared experience, pride, and a sense of family are tied to any specific task or goal. If sought after as intention, they can materialize today. If Sam and Debbie had set intentions rather than goals, they would have been living on the highs of fulfilling intention long after the ten-year mark. Instead, they were wondering, "What do we do now?"

For many couples, misery in a relationship sneaks up on them. It is often not something that happens as a result of one event or another. It is often the result of not seeking the lasting treasure of intention setting. I don't know if you have read the instructions on bottles of shampoo, but on almost every bottle, it gives these instructions: "Liberally apply shampoo to hair, lather, wait two minutes, and rinse. Repeat." What are you supposed to do for those four wasted minutes each morning? *Set your intentions!*

Each morning ask yourself, "What do I truly need or want today?" These answers will reveal your intentions. During the two minutes, set an "I am" intention and repeat it. Here are some truly helpful intentions that you can set if you are in a significant relationship or a marriage:

- I am a partner who listens
- I am accepting

The Couples Treasure Chest

- I am responsible
- I am loving and kind
- I am patient

These intentions will work to create satisfaction and joy in a relationship, even if you live in a cramped apartment and still have not bought a house. These intentions will work to create joy, even if your partner has different intentions. These intentions will bring joy, even if something comes along and diverts the plan. There is power in setting intentions; they are more important than goals.

In every relationship, people have those "Woulda, Coulda, Shoulda" moments where they realize they would do something different in the past if they had to do it over again. Setting intentions works even if you made poor choices, didn't save as much as you had hoped to, and even if things have gotten miserable. They work because each day, you can set a new intention. You can unlock this treasure in two minutes while shampooing your hair. The results are astounding.

What intention can you set right now? Can you set the intention to be joyful? Can you set the intention to be intimate? Can you set the intention to be honest? Not only can you do it, but you never have to wait to activate any of these intentions. You can step into it immediately despite outside experiences and even the choices of others.

Chapter Five
Positive Words

"I don't love you!" When Ezra first said it, she looked very cute, and Robert gazed into her eyes and leaned in for a kiss. Ezra pulled back, her eyes widened, and she then lunged forward and planted a kiss right on Robert's lips. Early in Robert and Ezra's relationship, this playful exchange occurred after a moment of passion, and it became their thing. Robert would say, "I love you," and Ezra would respond, "I don't love you." It was flirtatious and fun. It always ended with Ezra kissing Robert.

A few years into their relationship, Robert and Ezra came to me because they were feeling work-related stress as partners in a cook-it-yourself pizza franchise. When I asked about their relationship, this was one of the first stories they shared with me because they both thought it was so cute. As our session continued, it was clear they both were committed to the relationship, but I noticed a pattern in Ezra's communication. She would often communicate with words that expressed scarcity or negativity. When I asked them what they hoped to accomplish as a long-term goal, Ezra told me what they couldn't accomplish. When I asked her what being

Robert's partner was like, she playfully said, "I do all the work, he just talks to people." Again, she was being cute, and Robert understood this. Yet, I could sense a bit of insecurity on his part.

Many hurtful words are often spoken in a playful moment. Given a strong relationship, these words are most often taken as they are intended—a playful exchange of power in a relationship where joy is the usual norm. But any relationship will eventually experience lean time, times of stress, or unexpected transitions. It is in these moments that the years of playful negativity can suddenly cause doubt, insecurity, and hurt.

Jewel and Alex were another couple I worked with. They came to me in the midst of misery and were trying marriage counseling before they finally called it quits. A lot of couples do this. They want to be able to say they tried, and so they schedule a marriage counseling session even though they have made up their minds already. Jewel just didn't want to try anymore. She said that Alex's pattern of negativity made her too tired to go on.

Jewel described a pattern of ongoing putdowns and felt that Alex often discounted her thoughts and feelings. Robert responded to this with an emphatic, "That's not true, you are not being fair to me!" which is ironic, as

The Couples Treasure Chest

that is precisely what discounting someone's thoughts and feelings sounds like. Jewel retorted, "Remember when we were at Easter last year, and you told me my hat looked funny?" Robert was silent. "I still remember. It has been almost a year, and I have never worn a hat again!" Robert apologized, "I meant funny as in cute! I didn't know that upset you!"

In couples' communication, such exchanges are often par for the course. Negative words, spoken without ill intention, produce small cuts. Chances are that in any other relationship, Alex calling the hat "funny" would have been taken as meaning cute, but in this relationship, Jewel understood it as criticism because Alex had a pattern of negative word choices.

In any communication, the meaning of that interaction is the message the sender understands. Jewel had a long history of feeling insecure about her appearance, even long before her relationship with Alex started. Alex knew of her struggles with her parents, who she felt were always critical (they say we often marry someone like our own parents), and his words often made her feel like she was twelve years old again.

In many relationships, another pattern of negative communication exists. This is the pattern of negative interpretations; it occurs when one partner ascribes to the other a negative motivation or perception. An example might be one partner asking for help with the dishes after a particularly messy meal. The simple request, "Can you help me with the dishes?" is interpreted as, "You never do the dishes or help with anything, and I have to do all the work." The result is defensiveness and a response like, "You go sit down, *I* will do all the dishes. I do a lot around here!"

In this example, you can see defensiveness (and even overcompensation) occurred in the face of a simple request. For some couples, day-to-day communication can escalate into a fight. "I didn't say you don't do anything, I just asked if you would help me with the dishes," is the next response and now, a simple situation that most couples resolve without difficulty, can become World War 3.

Words are powerful. They can start a war. Literally. In international politics, words mean something. Many wars have been the result of escalating rhetoric. In business, wars can also begin from words. Rudolf and Adolf Dassler owned a shoe company in the 1930s, but when seeking refuge from Allied bombing, Rudolf and his wife sought shelter in a bunker. When Adolf and his wife joined them in the bunker, Rudolf explained, "The pigs are back!" (Rudolf later tried to explain he was talking about the British, not his brother and his wife.) By the end of World War 2, the brothers split their shoe company, entering a business rivalry that started with words. Adolf (Adi) became Adidas, and Rudolf started Puma. This rivalry between the two companies persists to this day, even though their founders have long since been dead.

Stop hunting for misery and hunt for treasure

In order to find treasure in your relationship rather than misery, negative words and negative patterns of communication must be smashed. The alternative to hunting for misery is to hunt for treasure by intentionally using positive language. You must be willing to go to any length to both find the positive in any relationship and to intentionally choose positive language. Perhaps the attitude here can be summed up by a popular internet meme: "Somebody called me pretty today! Actually, they said, 'You are pretty annoying,' but I chose to only focus on the positive."

Negative communication patterns include:

- Focusing on what is lacking or missing
- Criticism that starts with "You're…" or "You always…"
- Placing blame

- Contempt and sarcasm
- Defensiveness

There are many other negative communication patterns that couples may use, but these are the top five dealbreakers that lead to misery. It is important to note that even if you are correct in the facts of a matter, these five patterns can devastate the dynamics of a relationship. There is a better way. It is to use positive communication.

Let's take three simple words: Imagine, beautiful, and together.

These are three words that, on their own, are generally regarded as positive words. By choosing to use them intentionally, these powerful words shift the dynamic of communication. In and of themselves, using one of these words the right way won't fix a severely damaged relationship, but in a treasure chest, wealth comes from the collection of coins—rarely from just one of them.

Imagine

(Negative) "We need to buy better lawn furniture."

(Negative) "Our backyard is boring."

(Positive) "Imagine how awesome our backyard would be if we got some new lawn furniture."

Imagine is a powerful word. It causes somebody who hears it to take action. To visualize something, and that is the first step in changing anything.

Of course, one could string all three of these words together:

(Positive) "Imagine what it would be like if we had beautiful lawn furniture in our backyard to enjoy together!"

By using positive language in day-to-day scenarios, you are literally filling your relationship treasure chest. It promotes assertive communication, it is easier for the mind to process, and it fosters a spirit of cooperation. In fact, not only will your relationship benefit when you strive to use positive language, the whole family will. Words change our reality. They change our brain and our experience of being in a relationship.

Dr. Andrew Newberg and Mark Waldman of Thomas Jefferson University have researched the image of positive language. They write in *Words Can Change Your Brain*, "A single word has the power to influence the expression of genes that regulate physical and emotional stress," and "By holding a positive and optimistic [word] in your mind, you stimulate frontal lobe activity. This area includes specific language centers that connect directly to the motor cortex responsible for moving you into action. And as our research has shown, the longer you concentrate on positive words, the more you begin to affect other areas of the brain."

When you speak with positive language and positive words, you are sharing treasure. You are gifting your partner with something optimistic and hopeful that changes the brain, the response, the emotions, and the outcomes of your situation. It is worth noting that one positive word used today will probably not counteract years or even decades of negative communication, but treasure is often accumulated just as the misery was. By changing your language today, you produce results that can counteract the deficit of positivity.

What are some positive examples you can use today in your relationship?

Well, if there are obvious word choices, even if not intended to be hurtful, like "I don't love you," it is time to put those patterns and word choices away. Here are some examples of positive and optimistic communication in relationships.

"That is a good question" rather than "Why would you think that?"

The Couples Treasure Chest

"This could be a puzzle or a challenge" rather than "This won't work."

"What I can do is _____" rather than "I can't do that."

"My pleasure" rather than "No problem."

"I'm enjoying _____" rather than "I don't like this part."

"Sharing with you" rather than "Giving to you."

The idea here is that in your everyday word choices, you are looking for the positive, you are looking for words that emphasize teamwork or partnership, and you are validating your partner, even if you don't agree with everything.

Then, of course, some words simply exude positivity. These should become part of your daily vocabulary. You can take a dry erase marker and write this on your bathroom mirror so that they are the first thing you see each day, and you can try with intention to use these positive words. You could even create your own word list; the potential words on the list are innumerable.

- Share
- Discover
- Find
- Love

- Accept
- Grateful
- Beautiful
- Kind
- Affection
- Flourish
- Like
- Generous
- Captivating
- Team
- Partnership
- Aligned
- Thriving
- Vibrant
- Imagine

With intention, look for ways to communicate positively with positive words and phrases. Look at the treasure chest as being half full rather than half empty, and add new treasures to it. The rewards will be plentiful.

Chapter Six
Positive Emotions

Do you want your relationship to flourish? By the way, that is another great positive word. It is the word that best summarizes the academic study of positive psychology. People don't just want to be happy, they want to flourish, and in a joyful relationship, flourishing is both the result of finding treasure together and having that treasure.

Positive psychology focuses on the idea that wellness is not created in therapy simply by trying to eliminate problems, but also by creating flow and flourish. This branch of psychology recognizes that being able to naturally function in an optimal emotional state (flow) creates opportunity, satisfaction, emotional security, and helps a person to flourish.

Marriage and family therapists have been quick to adapt the ideas of positive psychology to counseling couples who want to move from misery to joy in their relationship. The good news is that, like our previous exercises, you can begin storing the treasure of positive emotion in your treasure chest with or without the immediate support of your partner. One of the things I have tried to focus on in this book is the strategies you can use independently of your partner's willingness to help. When relationships have moved into misery, that misery can be complacent, or it can be familiar and comforting in a paradoxical way. For this reason, when you decide to change and seek joy rather than subsist in misery, you may or may not have their full participation in your treasure hunt.

A lot of people believe that for the experience of misery to change, both parties in a marriage or relationship must be willing to change. While it is true that at some point you will need buy-in from your partner who will need to join you on this treasure hunt in order to have lasting success, many partners can take unilateral action and make significant changes both in themselves and in the context of the relationship. In other words, even if your partner never joins you on this journey by practicing the principles in this book, you will flourish and find treasure. It also means that when you change you, you also change them, knowingly or unknowingly, and create the best likelihood that they will eventually join you in this treasure hunt.

"You have got to be kidding me!" Tyler said with disbelief to Kennedy, his wife. "This rock is worth

$10,000, and you found it in our neighborhood park?" His eyes got bigger as he stared at the rock. Kennedy said enthusiastically, "It's part meteor! It's small, but it's a billion years old!" Tyler smiled. "Oh my God! I wonder how many $10,000 rocks I have just kicked off the sidewalk in my life?" Tyler questioned. "Why didn't I pay attention to your rock collecting hobby earlier and learn this too! I bet we could have made a fortune by now since I work at a construction site!"

Making changes using the techniques in this book will likely produce an awakening, much like Tyler's. In the story above, the treasure was right in front of him, but he did not realize it until there was so much treasure it was impossible to miss. By changing yourself, you will change other people. For some, these realizations come quickly, and for others, they come slowly.

What this means is that to create a joyful marriage—one with a full treasure chest—you must begin filling it whether your partner participates or not. Some of the ideas in this book require the participation of both parties, like the Treasure Chest Journal in chapter one. Still, many of these ideas are techniques you can implement today, even without full participation from others.

Dr. Richard K. Nongard

One of the most powerful techniques you can use in your quest for treasures is to generate positive emotions even when they are hard to create, or do not come as a natural option. The emotions you carry can create responses in the people around us. If you are negative, depressed, anxious, or irritated, these emotions will fill your treasure chest with negativity, and the bounty won't be valuable.

I know that it may be hard for you to feel genuine joy when things are miserable. It may also be true that in your current relationship, you have replicated the relationships that were modeled for you and that when you look back, your previous relationships and even childhood home were not places filled with joy.

It is important to recognize that we are often paralyzed by all-or-nothing thinking. We might think that we can either be joyful or miserable. But in reality, these emotions, as different as they are, can coexist. What this means is that even in misery, we can experience joy. When I was a kid, I was very close to both of my grandparents. They lived remarkable lives and remained healthy well into their 90s. I feel very fortunate because I had the best grandparents in the world, and I had them with me until I was in my mid-40s. A lot of people are not so lucky. By age 95, my grandmother's health took a

The Couples Treasure Chest

turn for the worse, and in the last weeks of her life, she said, "I just wish I could die!" Near the end of both of their lives (my grandmother passed away at 95, and my grandfather passed away at 98), they were suffering from a variety of serious health issues.

When my grandparents finally passed away, I felt both immense sadness and grief, but I also felt a sense of joy and gratitude for having had them in my life for as long as I did. Negative and positive emotions can coexist. This means that even in trying and difficult times, we can cultivate positive emotions. We can begin filling our treasure chest with positive emotions, even if they are not shared by our partner or are only an ember among the larger flames of difficulty.

What emotions can fill your treasure chest quickly?

- Gratitude
- Curiosity
- Happiness
- Cheerfulness
- Resilience
- Empathy

To find these emotions, you might have to really look. They can be hidden by difficulty, sadness, and other tough emotions. But if you have read up to this point, we know at least hope currently exists! Hope is a great starting point. Hope leads to security, which leads to joy.

The key is to start noticing what is right. Do you have a non-toothache today? What I mean by this question is to take the time to notice what is right, not what is wrong. We often only pay attention to our teeth if there is a problem. Our natural inclination is to often overlook what is right. In my work as a professional hypnotist, I often work with patients who struggle with chronic pain. They come to see me because they have exhausted medications as a solution, surgical attempts to find solutions, and probably even all the natural cures. When they come to me, they know exactly where the pain is, they know exactly what hurts, and they know the precise indicators that the pain is going to get worse.

When they come to my office for the first time, I never ask them about their pain. My first question is, "Tell me where you feel the best? What part of your body is most comfortable?" For years they have been answering questions about the pain from their doctors and nurses, but in all these years, they have seldom been asked about what feels good. For many of these patients, the question is startling. They have to consider it or contemplate it. The most common answer I get is, "I

The Couples Treasure Chest

don't know! I always feel bad! I forgot that somewhere might feel good!"

You can start generating awareness of positive emotions right now. Awareness of positive emotions creates more positive emotions. Your positive emotions will be noticed by your partner, either consciously or unconsciously. You know exactly how it feels to share space with your partner when they are negative. You also know how good it feels to share that space on the rare occasions they are in a good mood. Likewise, your partner is reading your misery level and will respond to your amplification of joy.

Another strategy is the "what if?" strategy. If you just can't find positive emotions, ask yourself, "What would it be like if I did feel happy? What would it be like?" In a previous chapter, we set intentions, so set the intent with an "I am" statement. For example, "I am grateful." It is amazing how, by setting an intention, we no longer have to look for gratitude because we will start to notice it. It is almost like you have a positive emotion-generating machine. Look for it. You will find it. This is like a strategy used in sports performance coaching, sales, and business called the "Fake it 'til you make it" strategy. By acting as if, or faking it, you will actually create a new positive emotion where there was not one before.

This works on a physical level. The old brain, the amygdala, is not smart. It cannot tell the difference between fantasy and fact. By just fantasizing about positive emotions, the brain will react as if they exist and flood your body with the chemicals and signals as if they were real. Once your brain creates this state, it is your state.

Try it now. Intentionally laugh. Even if you have to fake it, say, "Hahaha!" Intentionally smile, even if you don't feel like it, even if you feel silly. Do it. Laugh again. Let out another "Hahahaha!" and smile again. Stand up; you can stand and read. Bookmark this page with your finger so you don't lose your place and jump! Jump again and laugh when you do! Smile. Laugh again, even if it's a fake or forced, "Hahahahaha!"

Now check. In some way, at some level, what do you notice? Do you notice joy? Laughter? A sense of wellbeing? Your brain will follow the thoughts you create. Create positive emotions, and you will experience them. But the most amazing part of this is that positive emotions, like all emotions, are infectious. Your partner will catch them. If you enter the room where your partner is tense, stressed, or miserable, and you carry positive emotions, they will notice. Do this enough, and you will be a pleasure to be around. The results? More treasure for you and your partner, all because you understand the power of positive psychology and how to generate valuable treasures on an emotional level that you can store in your treasure chest.

If you have a willing partner, schedule time together to create, feel, and notice positive emotions. Set an intention together: Tonight, at dinner, we will share what we are grateful for. Tonight, before bed, rather than using the phone to check that last email, we will share security together. This is an amazing exercise. I often tell couples to combine this with a gazing technique. The technique is easy: simply sit in silence with your partner, gazing into their eyes. While you do this, set the intention to feel love, or acceptance, or commitment. Set aside all the wrongs that have been committed, the blames and faults that could be assigned to one partner or another, and sit in silence for a predetermined amount of time. One minute, three minutes, or five minutes. Just be. Gaze at each other. Share your intention with your partner. This will change you both. On its own, this gazing technique can reorder a relationship. It can create, amplify, and sustain positive emotions.

Dr. Richard K. Nongard

Chapter Seven
Positive Touch

The first of the five senses we develop is touch. We were born blind, seeing almost nothing. Watch a newborn, and you will see it rooting around for a nipple. The baby latches onto the nipple based on the sense of touch. The skin receptors in a newborn give this first sense a profound level of development early on. While touch is the most important sense to develop first, we almost always focus on vision as being the predominant sense we utilize.

Our bodies have an instant reaction to touch from another person. It lowers blood pressure, releases oxytocin (the love and pleasure hormone), and it increases relational intimacy. As relationships spiral into misery, one of the first casualties is often touch. There may be sex, as many couples who are miserable still function sexually, but daily non-sexual affirming touch is often absent.

Touch is a treasure, and the research shows that couples who touch find and store more treasure in their treasure chest. Touching can take many forms:

The Couples Treasure Chest

- Hand holding
- Foot massage
- Back or shoulder massage
- Nuzzling
- Stroking hair and/or face
- Restful touch with the hand
- Nose kisses
- Hugs
- Arms around each other
- Spooning
- Sitting shoulder to shoulder
- Laying on your partner
- Kissing
- Dancing
- Sitting on partner

In fact, there is actually an infinite number of ways to touch, but all of them produce a profound physical and mental response. For many couples, misery has moved to a point where physical touch does not occur naturally and comfortably. One of the side effects of misery is avoidance, not only of that which is emotional but also physical. To begin collecting treasure for your treasure chest, it is going to be up to you to reinitiate touch in the relationship. This touch should be frequent and natural, not invasive, and affirmational.

I instruct couples who have avoided touch to begin with simple touch. Rather than sitting across from your partner at the table, sit next to them. Simply let your bodies touch as if you were seatmates in a theater. I instruct the couple to touch in the car, simply putting your hand on the thigh of your seatmate. These are the kinds of touch that are natural and affirming, but not invasive or surprising.

I also tell almost every client I work with, no matter why they come to see me, to begin walking each day and measure their steps with a pedometer app. By walking, you are increasing physical activity, and the healthier our bodies are, the healthier our emotions are. Walking also provides a relaxed way for the couple to begin natural touch by holding hands. For some couples, this might be the first time they have held hands in a long time, but by taking a risk and reaching for your partner's hand, if even just a pinky hold, connection is reestablished.

When you have a willing partner who wants to collect treasure with you, I recommend combining physical touch with gazing. By sitting on a bed or even the floor together, and sitting cross-legged with the knees touching and hands being held, five minutes of gazing while touching can be an amazing time of discovery. It sounds too simple to transform a relationship. Couples

The Couples Treasure Chest

who are miserable and share this with their friends are often told, "It is going to be hard or difficult to make change." Couples in therapy are often told that they must master specific communication patterns or therapeutic processes, and that "It's a long road to lasting change." Yet, in my experience, intentional non-shaming, non-sexual touch (especially when combined with gazing) can do in minutes what sometimes takes months or years to accomplish in therapy.

This is not to negate the value of therapy or hard work in interpersonal communication or emotional reprogramming. It just means that there are many paths to collecting treasure, and both intentional touch and gazing can be fast ways to jumpstart the process of other difficult change. Touch is so powerful at both communicating and decoding emotions, that those with communication difficulties in parts of their marriage can overcome these difficulties quickly by making sure touch is a part of the therapeutic process.

In a 2009 study by DePauw University, researcher Matthew Hertenstein instructed volunteers to communicate emotions to strangers only through touch, and the receiver of the message was to decipher the emotion being shared. In up to 90% of the cases, powerful emotions were easily discerned by communicating only through touch. Do you want to open the door to love in your relationship? What about gratitude? Or Happiness? According to Hertenstein, this can all be accomplished through touch. Each time we touch our partner, we are adding another coin to the treasure chest of positivity.

The power of touch to change pursued, and the ability to create connections even extends from marriages and romantic relationships to almost any type of human interaction. Have you ever been browsing a product packaged in a cardboard box that also has a cutout so you can tough the product inside? Touch leads to increased sales. In retail sales, products displayed in a way that permits touching dramatically increases sales over no-touch displays. Even a touch screen can increase sales or positive responses to messages. In trade shows, booths with touch screens drive both an increase in traffic and extend the time a potential prospect will be engaged.

Seek out opportunities to touch. You can place a hand on your partner's shoulder, you can pat them on the back or stroke an upper arm. You can choose to sit next to them or on them. All of these interactions will add a few more coins to the treasure chest and communicate the emotions you might not be able to find words to say.

The Couples Treasure Chest

Because touch is such a powerful way of communicating, during difficult times, your touch might be rejected. Be prepared for this response. Listen to your partner, and if they find touch intrusive and express that, respect it. But the chances are, they will accept your touch because subconsciously they too want connection, or they would already be gone.

There is something else you can do to foster positive emotions in difficult times. You can touch yourself. I teach my clients a simple strategy for managing anxiety called the 3-2-1 Emotional Reset Technique. Self-touch increases oxytocin, releases endorphins, and can make a huge difference in helping you find positive emotions in difficult times. Change begins with yourself, and this strategy can be a wonderful strategy to help you add your fair share to the treasure chest.

It is called the 3-2-1 Emotional Reset Technique because there are three steps. The second step focuses on touch.

To begin, find a comfortable place; you can be seated or standing. What is most important is you turn off distractions, such as computer windows that might call your attention, or turn off the phone or smartwatch. The reason this is important is that in self-hypnosis, even with a quick process like this, we should become dedicated to it. Distractions are like a tap on the shoulder—we can't not turn around to see who it is. So it is always best to minimize these even if only for a few moments.

Step One: As you read these words, simply scan your body, and release any obvious tension you are holding on to and pay attention to your breath. As you pay attention to your breath, count the next three breaths. You can do this with your eyes open if you are reading. Accessing the resource state of self-hypnosis is not dependent on the eyes being open or closed.

You do not have to breathe in any special way. You can breathe quickly or slowly. You can breathe deeply if you want to, but the most important thing is to just breathe and to count the three breaths. This step is all about grounding and being present in this moment.

Step Two: Take your two hands and cross them across your upper body, placing the left hand on the right upper arm, and the right hand on the left upper arm. This is almost a self-hug. It feels pretty good to hug yourself, and in yoga practices, this is advocated because it connects our physical experience to our inner experience. The research actually shows that this self-hug position can trigger physiological responses and release the chemicals in the brain associated with pleasure, security, and wellbeing. At this point, you can also touch your upper arms with your fingertips, moving them in a figure eight, as if you were petting yourself or giving yourself a gentle massage.

Some therapists who practice methods of bilateral stimulation also believe that by crossing the left side to the right side, we are integrating our thinking and feeling mental capacities.

Step Three: Spend the next one minute (three breaths, two hands, one minute) and practice paying attention to the breath. Be an observer of the breath. You can do this with the eyes open or the eyes closed. What is most important is that you allow your breath to be a focal point. Each breath marks each moment. By practicing staying in the present, you are setting aside regrets of the past or fears of the future. During this minute, your mind will continue to think. After all, this is what minds do. Like a fish swims in water, people swim in thoughts. Thinking is perfectly okay. So is being aware of emotions, and so is noting physical sensations.

The practice that you are trying to cultivate during this minute is not stopping your thoughts, emotions, or sensations, but rather practicing not following them and using them as a cue to return your attention to the present moment.

You can use a timer, or you can just guesstimate when a minute has passed by. It is also perfectly okay to spend more than a minute focusing on the power of this moment. When you are ready to open your eyes, let a smile come to your face and release your self-hug. You can congratulate yourself now. You have just done your first self-hypnosis exercise!

This is a very basic process but a highly effective one. By adding nothing to this process and simply using it to stop anxiety, practice mindfulness, and relax, it will be of value and serve you well for years to come. I have taught this to countless clients, and I have never had anyone exclaim, "OMG Richard! That was amazing! You changed my life! Thank you!" Rather, when I teach this to people, they typically have the same response you probably have. They say things like, "Okay, I can see how that is helpful." Or they say, "That was relaxing." Or simply, "Okay, I did it."

I wish that for most of my clients, the power of this technique was revealed in the first practice. What happens far more often is that when I tell my clients to practice this twice a day for the next two weeks, they come back with what I call "retrospective excitement." By practicing it, they realize the profound value in it.

Self-hypnosis is a practice. Like a musician who must practice her instrument before a debut concert or a comedian who must memorize his scripts and practice his timing to make it appear spontaneous and natural, self-hypnosis requires practice. You will need to be committed to this practice to derive the results, but I promise you the results can be profound.

Dr. Richard K. Nongard

Chapter Eight
Invest in Time

Warren Buffet, perhaps the world's most famous investor and richest man, famously said, "The poor invest in money, the rich invest in time." In the world of investing, Buffet is known for the strategy of "buy and hold," which refers to not tracking daily movements in stock price and recognizing that wealth comes from the length of time a stock is held. In relationships, a corollary might be, "Time heals all wounds."

It is interesting to note how time is an important measure not only in a relationship or investing but in other areas of life. Many have claimed that mastery of any craft, skill, or habit requires 10,000 hours for proficiency. An airline pilot who has 10,000 hours is considered an experienced expert; a musician who has practiced 10,000 hours is considered a top performer. Ten thousand hours is about five to seven years of full-time practice. I have been learning how to speak Mandarin, now that I am in my third year of study, and we speak Chinese in our home daily, so I am probably coming up on 10,000 hours of study and practice. The result is that intuitively I no longer have to translate in my head and can now think in Mandarin.

I am acquainted with an elderly couple that has a tumultuous marriage, now going on 40 years. For both of them, it was a second marriage. When they got married and combined families in the 1970s, it was supposed to be like *The Brady Bunch* but ended up much more like the scary episodes of *The Twilight Zone*. They were products of a time when divorce was rarely an option, and many problems strained the relationship. It is through perseverance, and now, in their twilight years, that compassion rules the day, love can be seen, and time has yielded its rewards.

Fortunately, to move from misery to joy, you don't have to wait 40 years. The couple just referenced employed no marriage counseling and sought no strategies for change. The lesson from them is that time does, in fact, yield treasure, but by implementing the ideas in both previous and upcoming chapters of this book, you will be able to fill your treasure chest faster. You have almost certainly already tried some of these strategies and are now yielding at least some results.

The strategy that is at the core of this chapter is universal in business, marriage, parenting, and task mastery. It is the strategy of spending time doing something valuable.

As a family therapist, I have worked with many children and their parents. I have heard parents justify a lack of involvement with their children by saying, "It the quality of time that is important." But my work with children does not validate this belief. Children get that time is important, and a parent who only spends "quality" time with a kid communicates a powerful message: "You are worth less than my time."

In marriage and couples' relationships, this is also true. I meet couples who believe that they spend quality time together but are limited in the time they can spend together because of work, other relationships, travel, or even because other important tasks like parenting can cause them to divide time or be limited in time. In reality, time spent with a partner creates mastery in a relationship, just as it does in any other endeavor. Simply being with your partner is valuable, even if the time together is not spent doing anything of significance. Let's tackle the big deals first: going to bed at the same time and sharing a meal.

Sharing a bedtime can be difficult for some couples. Circadian rhythms (our internal clocks) regulate our feelings of wakefulness and sleepiness. For some couples, their internal clocks just don't match. For other couples, work obligations or other tasks (one getting up earlier to care for children or go to work) can also impact sleeping times. Many other things can get in the way of couples sharing a bedtime, but happy couples find a way to reset their internal clocks or rearrange priorities so that bedtime can be shared. One positive benefit of this shared schedule is the likelihood of increased sexual activity since a shared bedtime makes intimacy easier.

Research shows that couples who go to sleep at the same time have fewer arguments, better sleep, and feel a stronger emotional connection. As a partner looking for ways to store treasure, this can add a few gold bars to your treasure chest. The difference between sleeping at the same time or going to bed at different times can be huge. You should find a way to make this happen. Discuss with your partner how to work towards it, and if you truly want to experience joy, prioritize it.

Mealtime is another shared experience where simply attending to each other by sharing time can have a powerful impact. Chances are pretty good that your relationship began with shared meals. For many couples, the first date was lunch or dinner. For a couple who met at school or work, it may have been those shared meals that fostered the friendship and eventual relationship.

Eating together won't only make your relationship better, it will even make your food taste better! Couples who ate together rated their meal as better almost 20% of the time, and 40% of those who ate alone enjoyed their meal less. When couples eat together, they stay together. They are more likely to converse, more likely to learn about their partner, and more likely to share details of life that foster intimacy and connection.

It may seem too simple to say that if couples just spend time eating together and going to bed at the same time that a miserable marriage can improve, but that is what the facts say. It is often the simple things that make significant differences. Years ago, a book caught my attention because of the title: *Sex Begins in the Kitchen*. The idea is, of course, that shared time increases every aspect of intimacy. In the kitchen, cooking and even cleaning together creates cooperation. My grandparents were married for over 75 years. My grandfather used to say the reason they lasted so long is that they did the dishes together every night. She washed, he dried them and put them away. What was really valuable was the time they spend together.

Couples can carve out time together by sharing activities. Anything from washing the car to washing the dog. I have to confess, I am not an avid car washer. Twice a year is good enough for me. My wife, on the other hand, is a weekly car washer. After we got married, she would drive to the $3 car wash and wash and vacuum the cars each week. It is not a task I particularly enjoy nor one I find important. At some point, though, I felt guilty and went with her to "do my part." She still does all the work, but I have found that the time spent doing a mundane task makes us both a little happier. I am the same about washing the dog. She wants to wash the dog a lot. I guess you can tell who the slob in this relationship is! But I recognize that it's not only about sharing the workload but also about spending time together, and so I now wash the dog with her.

It is important to carve out time with your spouse, even watching TV and sitting in the same room. This time communicates something powerful. It communicates, "I value simply being with you." In addition to carving out small blocks of time in the day, couples should also look for the ability to find extended time together. Driving and exploring the countryside for an afternoon, visiting interesting local places together, and seeking a bit of adventure can also provide ways to spend time with your partner.

Americans spend more than 100 billion dollars a year on just summer vacations. Vacations are a great way to spend extended time together, but adding to financial burden is not the way to do it. This can cause difficulty far beyond the rewards of spending time together. If a vacation is in the cards for you, seek an affordable vacation; Discount Vegas getaways can be an amazingly affordable adventure (far less then the average cost of a family vacation due to flight deals and hotel discounts). But local vacations to a rented lake cabin or even just a camping trip to a state park can be affordable fun vacations.

You can also find time to spend with your partner by scheduling your time with them. You schedule your work and your other responsibilities. Block time off on your calendar for your partner. The results will increase your romantic wealth. As you spend time with your partner, increase the quality of that time. You can increase the quality by being curious about them and their interests, and you can increase your conversations by looking for connection and using the positive language choices illustrated in a previous chapter.

Another aspect of this is that it is important to enjoy the time and seek activities and ways to spend time together doing that which is enjoyable. During the COVID-19 pandemic, one couple I worked with, Marty and Garth, began playing Pickleball. Garth told me that he and his spouse didn't even know what pickleball was until, while watching the news, the governor had closed most public facilities except outdoor sports facilities. Marty thought, *What the heck is Pickleball?* and immediately went to a search engine, which let to an online shopping site, and within four days, four Pickleball paddles and six balls showed up on their doorstep.

Marty told me, "Neither of us are particularly athletic, but it got us out of the house and doing something fun." Marty continued, "We are not any good, but it has been a great way to spend time together, and we met a few of our neighbors who also discovered Pickleball." If you and your partner develop common interests, it will naturally produce more shared time. Seek out opportunities to learn new places to go, activities to do, and ways to increase that time together in situations where conflict can be kept to a minimum.

Dr. Richard K. Nongard

Chapter Nine
Live in the Present

The Great Master Oogway profoundly said, "Yesterday is history, tomorrow is a mystery, but today is a gift...that is why it is called the present." These words, from the turtle in the movie *Kung-Fu Panda*, have, perhaps, the greatest ability to make your life better than any other truth uttered by any other philosopher. How can words spoken by a cartoon turtle in a kid's movie make your marriage better? Master Oogway was teaching the core concept of mindfulness—a proven strategy for controlling stress, decreasing emotional pain, and navigating difficult life situations.

More importantly, Mindfulness-Based Relationship Enhancement (MBRE) has proven to help couples store the treasure they seek. It can eliminate jealousy, foster forgiveness, and promote feeling secure in your relationship. MBRE focuses on how to just be, despite change, difficulty, or problems. It promotes healthy acceptance of your current situation, even if there is still more work to do. It also promotes relaxation and broadening your self-awareness. All of these promote healthy relationships and can add treasure to your treasure chest.

Volumes of research, countless TEDx talks (I did a TEDx talk on mindfulness in Oklahoma City), and mental health clinics specializing in training patients in mindfulness all prove one thing: The turtle was right. Are you familiar with the Serenity Prayer? It is a popular prayer in the self-help community and can directly apply to help you store treasure. The part of the prayer that scares people is the part that says, "Grant me the courage to accept the things I cannot change." Nobody likes this part of the prayer.

Mindfulness gives us a solution to this discomfort, and in dealing with your spouse, the children, and even extended family, there is a lot you will never be able to change. You might never see a change in others' destructive behavior. You might never get your spouse on board with addressing issues that really are their responsibility to resolve. You may never be able to move more than 50 miles away from where you live, no matter what opportunity presents itself.

But don't stop reading. I am about to give you the details of how Master Oogway's words can be translated into life-changing strategies that can turn the present moment—no matter how tough—into a gift. Suspend your disbelief for a moment. I know I have made an extravagant claim, but let me explain how this magic works and what to do. If you painstakingly pay attention to these instructions and practice the strategy I share until it becomes second nature, from this point forward, situations that used to upset you will be handled intuitively in a way that actually transforms your trauma and makes life better.

Are you worried about your children? The good news is that when parents master mindfulness as a stress-reduction strategy, they have better marriages and more resilient children. A study by Ortiz and Siblinga shows that children with adverse childhood experiences (parental divorce is considered a major adverse childhood experience and a predictor of many later-in-life difficulties) who are taught mindfulness cultivate an ability to handle not only this adversity but other adversities with resilience. In other words, they come through emotional stories that destroy others, and they can put the broken pieces of their lives back together when others just fall apart. Again, another extravagant promise. But it's a promise made with mountains of research behind it. ACT Therapy, developed by Steven Hays at the University of Nevada; Mindfulness-Based Stress Reduction, developed by Jon Kabat-Zinn at the University of Massachusetts; and Dialectical-Behavioral

Therapy, studied by Marsha Linehan at the University of Washington, are all research-backed approaches to master the art of Master Oogway's words—and study after study shows that they work.

Do I have your attention now? Are you feeling a little more hopeful that you can deposit treasure in your couple's treasure chest by mastering mindfulness? Here is how it works:

Master Oogway said, "Yesterday is history" to highlight an essential truth: The past is what it is, and the past cannot be changed. If we could change the past, I bet most of us would make substantial changes. But we can't. And this regret is a source of much of our pain. Our natural tendency, both consciously and subconsciously, is to dwell in the regret of the past—even to ruminate about poor choices we made—in addition to the poor choices others made. Put in the context of marriage problems, we might regret our previous interactions with our partner, maybe even regretting that we gave them the benefit of the doubt, and it just made matters worse. Or maybe, you are wishing you could unblend a blended family, and you look at your wedding pictures, knowing today that you would not do it over again but that breaking it all apart actually won't fix that mistake either.

Dr. Richard K. Nongard

The past is another mind trap. Many of us expend mental energy ruminating over the past. Why do we do that? There is a good reason why we torture ourselves with revisiting and mentally reliving the past with woulda, shoulda, couldas. That reason is evolutionary biology and our brains. Our brains are wired to scan out the past to tell us what to do today. The brain gives us information so we can take quick action and navigate difficult situations—but this skill was not developed to help us deal with step-spouse issues. It was developed, over millions of years, to help us overcome natural disasters and to catch prey and protect villages. In the past, there were no weather forecasters warning of impending tornadoes, hurricanes, and natural disasters. In the past, there were no grocery stores; if you didn't catch the food fast enough, and it ran away, your entire village might perish over the winter.

Do you see the point here? It is natural for us to dwell on the past and litigate previous experiences because it gives us a basis of knowledge for action at the most basic of all survival instinct levels. But couples' problems are unique to our modern world, and our brains have yet to adapt in a meaningful way to these new situations, so we regret the past and feel pain but have no solution.

Master Oogway's simple words are telling us to stop ruminating and start living. Eventually, Oogway tells us exactly how to do that. But first, he warns us of another mind trap by saying, "Tomorrow is a mystery." Our brilliant minds, which help us store and quickly retrieve information to catch prey and save the village, also tend to scan the future to anticipate disaster. The evolutionary mind protects us by projecting and predicting disaster. When it is not looking back and drawing on experience, it is looking ahead and guessing what will come next. And if you lived 50,000 years ago, and there were no weather forecasters, this strategy might have protected you as you anticipated how to protect your village from natural disasters and an Ice Age.

But again, in the modern world, it serves little utility. Holding your phone and stalking your step-spouse's social media so you can predict what your spouse's mood will be later that day is not a wise use of mental energy. Not sleeping at night because you lay your head on the pillow and, in the quiet of the night, begin to anticipate all the nasty things they might do—the court filings they could harass you with, and the misery you might feel next month at a high school graduation (when you must all be together again)—is not a wise use of mental energy.

Fortunately, most of what we worry about actually never happens (numerous university studies have demonstrated this) even when our minds make these fears logical and realistic. This is why Oogway's words are so important—despite our mind's attempts to make our anxieties worth worrying about, the fact is, they are not worth worrying about.

This idea of mindfulness is not an idea just from Master Oogway; Jesus preached on this in the book of Matthew, saying, "Why do you worry? Do you not see how God cares for the lilies of the field? How much more important are you to him." It is reflected in ancient Buddhism, with the idea that by being mindful, we can set aside the regrets of the past and the fears of the future and live in the present.

The value of living in the present, rather than with past regrets or in future fears, is that it is the only moment that we have control over. Each breath marks a new moment. And in each new moment, we have an opportunity; that opportunity is to let a thought, a feeling, or an emotion just be a thought, a feeling, or an emotion without having to follow it. Following these thoughts, feelings, and emotions is what brings us back to past regrets or pushes us into future fears.

This is why mindfulness practitioners find a focal point (often the breath) to bring their attention to when they find their mind ruminating over the past or projecting into the future.

When Oogway said, "…but today is a gift," he was giving us the code that can break these destructive patterns of obsession, fear, grief, pain, anxiety, anger, and any other set of unresourceful emotions or behaviors we engage in. I am actually typing these words on my laptop on an airplane. There is some bad weather, and the flight was delayed due to storms. Now that it has taken off, it's a bit bouncy. If you were on this plane with me, you would probably notice some people looking pretty nervous. In their minds, they are probably noticing their fear and following it to all the "what-ifs" that the mind can possibly create. Some of them are probably even mentally revising their will or watching images of their children at their funeral.

But what is the reality here? The reality here is that no matter how turbulent the flight is, as long as you are breathing, you are okay. I work with oncology patients in therapy. Some of them have catastrophic diagnoses, but I tell them that as long as they are breathing, they are okay. In these two examples, the real problem comes when you stop breathing. And that could happen at some point. But until then, stay in this moment, no matter how bad things seem to be, and oddly, this simple strategy changes everything. It creates resilience, builds patience, increases acceptance, gives us space between us and our emotions, and lets us quell poor decision-making.

This is what you need right now. It will turn the present into a gift: the gifts of serenity and maybe, acceptance. Right now, your relationship is making you miserable. But the gift of mindfulness is best used to put some emotional space between your thoughts and emotions. When this happens, unlike the prehistoric mind that will be scanning the past and projecting into the future, the new mind will find clarity, meaning, and even discover how something good can come out of a situation that is so tragic.

You wanted a love story, but you got a difficult relationship—a husband or wife that won't address the issues, and your worst fears about what will happen to you if you are dragged any deeper into the conflict. Where is the love? Like our breath, it is still there. And mindfulness can help you bring it back to the present. It will give you hope. And even though things may be different than you expected, just like the people on my turbulent airplane, as long as you are breathing, you are okay too.

On my website at CouplesTreasure.com, I will give you some free resources to learn and practice mindfulness. Just tell me where to send your access, and I will expound on the strategy below. But even if you don't take this skill to the next level, you can find that by practicing the following mental exercise daily, you can switch off old patterns of thinking and feeling and open a new pathway to staying sane amid the difficulty and drama.

How to Practice Mindfulness

Mindfulness is a skill. It is something that is not intuitive since it requires retraining the prehistoric mind and creating new patterns. The good news, though, is that the practice is not hard, and it does not take a long time. You can practice these instructions for three to four minutes two or three times a day for 21 days, and you will then be amazed at the results. When I first teach this to clients in my therapy office, they say things like, "Well, that was relaxing," or "I can see how that could help." But they never have a profound response. The profound response comes when you make mindfulness your new default mental pattern, and that comes through practice. The result? On Day 22, after three weeks of short daily practice, when your step-spouse passes a passive-aggressive message to you through the children (such as when your step-kids say, "But my mom says you…"), you will find that you respond with mindfulness rather than regret or anxiety, or serenity and love rather than anger.

Practicing mindfulness will allow you to sleep at night when you learned of a court action on a Friday afternoon but can't speak to your attorney until Monday morning. Practicing mindfulness will help you notice hope, even where there has been pain, and will help you detach from emotions you previously used to be enmeshed by.

To do this basic mindfulness practice, find a spot where you can sit for two to three uninterrupted minutes. Turn off your phone; this is *your* time.

Now, begin to pay attention to your breath. Really study the breath, noticing what it feels like to breathe the air in and out. Ask yourself what the breath feels like, and follow the air in and out. You do not need to breathe in any special way; this is not yoga, so just breathe and pay attention to the breath. Of course, each breath marks each moment, which is the only time we really have.

Take the next two minutes to practice the skill anytime you notice a thought, a feeling, or even a physical sensation. Simply acknowledge that emotion (Say to yourself, "That was anger," or "That was fear."), but rather than following it, use it as a cue to turn your attention back to your breath. What you are doing here is breaking the pattern of following an emotion into the past or the future and staying in the present (the breath). Do not judge the emotion. It does not matter if it is good or bad or something you do or don't like. What matters is that you are practicing how to break the cycle of following this emotion and amplifying your pain.

Do the same thing with your thoughts ("I hate my partner today," or "I wish I never remarried.") and practice letting a thought be a thought without judging it. No need to makes sense out of your thoughts; just say to yourself, "Wow! Another thought." And use it as a cue to return your attention to your breath.

You can do this with your sensations as well (the tension in your body, pain in your shoulders, the stress in your brow, etc.), and when you become aware of them, do not try to get rid of them; just try to bring your attention back to your breath.

You may think that there are too many thoughts, emotions, or sensations. You might find yourself returning your attention to your breath hundreds of times in a short couple of minutes. That is okay. Like a fish swims in water, people swim in thoughts. You are not trying to not think or not feel or not sense. That would be abnormal. It really is impossible to "clear the mind, and think of nothing." What is possible is that you practice putting some space between you and your thoughts, feelings, and senses by practicing these techniques.

Take a minute and practice the above few paragraphs. Then repeat this twice a day every day for 21 days. I promise you that your life will be different from this point forward. It's simple, but it's profound.

And check out my web page; I want to make sure you have the resources that can help you. I have created a short course and some downloadable resources you can access for free. The website is CouplesTreasure.com

Chapter Ten
Cultivate Good Relationship Habits

Good relationship habits help you find treasure along your journey. Habits are things that we do automatically and intuitively; they are our first response in any situation. Habits develop over time and require practice. This means each of the eleven habits that happy couples do are habits you must begin with intention and continue to practice even when it feels like it is not working. Have you ever bought a shoe that you loved, but it took a few tries for it to become comfortable? This is what cultivating habits are all about: trying them on, practicing, and then stepping into them automatically as a first response.

Give Compliments

Happy couples give compliments. Couples who are miserable have often cultivated the habit of putdowns and harsh words. Using kind words and compliments is a new habit that we must develop in order to find treasure. Compliments are kind words, not simply flattery, and they come from the heart. Of course, during difficult times the adage, "If you can't say anything nice, don't say anything at all" works well when trying to break the old habit of defensiveness or criticism. Today, set the intention to say something kind, to give a compliment to your partner, and to be positive. The dividends in developing this habit are huge.

Public Affection

When you let others know that you value your partner, your partner will feel valued. You can do this by cultivating the habit of public affection. Holding hands, putting your arm around your partner, or giving a kiss when going in different directions communicates something powerful to your partner—that you are proud to be with them and appreciate them. In many cultures, public affection is suppressed, and couples in conflict often suppress the need for affection as well. Since I am assuming that you are reading this and live in a culture where affection is well-tolerated, go for it!

Practice Assertive Communication

Assertive people get what they want. If you want joy, ask for it! It really is that simple. By practicing assertive communication in every situation, you communicate clearly, misunderstandings are reduced, and compatibility is enhanced. I teach every client I know the following formula sentence:

I Feel-Want-Need _____.

This sentence breaks the pattern of passive communication where you hope your partner recognizes your needs and feelings, the patterns that passive-aggressive communication defensiveness and insecurity produce, or aggressive communication that simply runs over the needs of others.

Because the sentence begins with "I," the sentence is about you, and this can avoid conflict. When you clearly identify your feelings, wants, or needs, there is no ambiguity. It is clear. The blank is filled in by whatever it is that you feel, want, or need, and ends with a period. In other words, nothing else needs to be said. You can now wait for a response.

Practice this simple strategy for assertiveness, and you will quickly notice new responses from your partner and a new feeling of confidence in your own life. The bonus to this sentence is that you can use it at work, with your friends and children, and anywhere in life to live a more effective and fulfilling life.

Dr. Richard K. Nongard

Practice Psychological Flexibility

Psychologists who study misery, anxiety, fear, depression, and any other myriad of negative emotions almost always come to the same conclusion: Psychological flexibility is key. This is the heart of resilience, a concept so important that the U.S. military has spent millions of dollars researching ways to help soldiers develop psychological flexibility and manifest resilience. It has proven to be a solution to some of the problems associated with PTSD, and in some cases, a way of preventing the development of post-traumatic stress entirely (in situations where its development was the norm).

How is psychological flexibility developed? By making hope a verb and by using hope as a strategy. It pulls us out of our depression, stops our fear in its tracks, and makes a miserable situation a little bit better by refocusing one's attention on the desired result and the probability of achieving it. This does not mean that every aspect of life will be peaches and cream, but it does mean that by activating hope as a bridge from misery to acceptance, or from fear to confidence, that we have avoided making things worse.

When we stop making things worse, there is only one way for things to go; they start to improve. For some,

The Couples Treasure Chest

the transformation in their marriage is rapid and profound, and for others, slower and less intense. However, this reality will always materialize for those who use hope as a strategy, practice acceptance, and develop psychological flexibility.

Acceptance does not mean we like something, and it does not mean we hope it happens again. Rather, acceptance is the simple recognition that bad things have happened, they were painful, but that the past is history, and the present moment is where we must live. By cultivating acceptance, you will be cultivating psychological flexibility.

It takes practice to move to acceptance automatically, especially if the past has been particularly hurtful, but it is entirely possible. We can cultivate this acceptance by practicing mindfulness, living in the present moment, and forgiving. When it comes to forgiveness, we must practice this aspect of acceptance by forgiving both ourselves and our partners.

Practice Listening

A lot of us are not natural listeners. It has been said that "silence is golden." In relationships, silence can bring gold to your treasure chest. When I listen to couples fight, what I often hear are two people who are in agreement and even want the same outcomes, but because they are plotting their next counterpoint when their partner is speaking, they never listen. I am amazed at how often couples share the same desire, but they simply do not listen to each other.

Not listening comes from a place of scarcity thinking—the belief that if I listen, I won't get to speak or say my peace. Years ago, I had a friend who wrote a small book on theatrical theory and audience involvement in close-up magic. He had a chapter in his book with the chapter title "Silence." The rest of the page was simply blank, and when the page was turned, the next chapter began. His point was that silence gives us a chance to listen. When we listen, we cultivate treasure. This treasure comes in the form of understanding, empathy, and compassion. Seek every opportunity to listen.

Guiguzi, also known as the Sage from Ghost Valley, was an ancient Chinese philosopher on political matters. He noted that listening also provides a competitive edge in negotiation. Relationships are negotiations. He said, "Listen to your opponent as if you are a tongue seeking the marrow in the center of the bone." By listening, we don't have to guess what the opposition wants, we might find ourselves in a more powerful position, and we can discover the true wants, needs, and feelings of others.

The Couples Treasure Chest

Walk with Your Partner

We are only able to function as well emotionally as we are physically well. If you have been managing stress in your relationship and other areas of life, one of the best cures for that stress is increasing your physical activity. It's said that the best medication for high blood pressure is "sweat." In other words, increased physical activity makes us well, both physically and mentally.

The good news is that in the modern era, every cell phone has a pedometer app. If for some reason it is not built into your phone, you can download one for free. I encourage couples to download the pedometer app and walk together every day. They say 10,000 steps a day is a good target, but even walking for ten minutes and a thousand steps can have significant benefits.

I share with couples that the habit of walking together and creating a common goal in their daily step target can make a significant difference. Walking also gives an opportunity for listening, an opportunity for touching, and an opportunity for being together. There is perhaps no better habit for a couple to engage in than walking together on a daily basis.

These six habits will make a huge change in your relationship. Practice them and seek opportunities to use them. Practice makes perfect, and by engaging with intention in these six things, the result will be joy and a treasure chest filled with loot. Talk to your partner about this list. If both of you look for treasure together, you will fill up the treasure chest even faster.

Chapter Eleven
Cashing in Your Treasure

In any marriage, hard times will come. For Dan and Mia, the relationship started with hard times. Dan and Mia were high school sweethearts who planned to get married after college, but sometime during their senior year, Mia became pregnant. Young and broke with a baby on the way, they never got married—at first because they didn't have extra cash for a marriage license and then because constant difficulty and fighting had them at odds. They only stayed together because they had nowhere else to go, and both of them loved their son.

Dan was depressed. Years earlier, he started a small injection molding company with an old machine he purchased at an auction. He started making products for a growing auto parts supplier, and Mia was at his side. They spent too much time working, too much time just surviving, and little time looking for any treasure in their relationship, other than actual treasure in the form of paid invoices. Mia helped him with organizing the office and making sales calls, and the business grew, but so did the debt. Dan added equipment, employees, and they eked out enough cash to buy a house, pay their bills, and take care of their now growing family.

Dan and Mia never intended to be miserable; they intended to be in love. But the years of hard work, long hours, and different interests drove them apart. The disagreements turned into anger and the anger turned into minor irritations, which then developed into blow-out fights. They were together because they owned a business; the business never thrived, and neither did their relationship. Both were miserable. They were over ten years into both the business and their relationship when I met them.

Jeff came to a seminar I was giving on sales leadership when I shared the value of setting intention in sales. In my talk, I shared the value of setting intention rather than goals. This resonated with Jeff, and during the break, he said, "You're a therapist…how did you get into sales training?" I told him that in therapy, we are really doing sales—selling the idea that depressed people can find joy, that stressed people can find serenity, and that without buy-in, clients were stuck. In therapy, just like business-to-business sales, we have to close the deal by getting the client to buy in to making changes. I told him that I used the same ideas on setting intentions with couples that I do with salespeople. "Well, it seems my wife and I"— Jeff interrupted himself—"…well, we actually never got married. We make each other miserable. I don't intend to be miserable, but every day is just really tough. I wonder what would happen if we just intended to be nice to each other."

"You might find treasure," I replied.

"Treasure? We barely pay the bills," Dan said with frustration.

It was at this point that I shared with Dan the idea of the treasure chest. He got it. He understood the power it held. Dan thanked me for the idea, and of course, I went back to organizing handouts and answering some questions that other people had. It is not uncommon when I am giving a talk for people to come up to me during the break about other issues. Rarely do I hear from these participants again; after all, I travel to do these seminars, and I am usually only in town a couple of days.

It was about a year after meeting Dan that I got an email from him. He was writing to thank me for the great talk, and that even though his business was about the same, his relationship was doing great! He wrote in the email that for the past year, they had each written in the Treasure Chest book every day and that they were actually on book number two. He just wanted me to know.

I called Dan when I got this email. He said that even though his business wasn't making him rich, his relationship was. I shared with Dan a few of the other ideas in that call that I have shared in this book, and since I was going to be in town for another training in the near future, I asked if we could meet up for dinner with his wife. I wanted to hear from her how this one idea made a difference.

At dinner, Mia shared some of the hardships they had and how they were ready to call it quits when Dan came home with this "stupid treasure chest idea." She laughed as she called it stupid. "I really thought it was stupid, but I figured if he wanted to do it, I would try. At first, I really couldn't think of anything nice to say about Dan. But I tried. At first, I only wrote a word or two. After all, this was his idea." Mia looked at me. "I didn't know Dan really valued me. That book changed everything. It seemed like Dan could write things, even if he didn't speak them to me. And I started smiling."

This is the power of the treasure chest. It's a simple idea, but it is sometimes the simple things that can make profound changes.

The Couples Treasure Chest

In this book, I have shared a lot of ideas. Some of them might make a huge difference right away and move you quickly from misery to joy, and some of these might add a few coins to the treasure chest over time. None of these ideas will fail. All of them, big and small, have one thing in common: If you don't try them, everything will stay the same.

The flip side is true also. If you do try them when hard times come again—and in life, they always will—there will be a wealth of treasure to sustain during difficult times. Dan and Mia eventually did close their business, and Dan took a job with a former competitor. Mia ended up going to cosmetology school, something she had put off for years. During these transitions, more hard times came, but unlike the previous hardships that drove them to misery, they now found themselves drawing closer together. They finally felt like a couple and were married in Las Vegas last year. Their son was their best man.

In this book, you have learned seven keys to help you find treasure in your relationship. Each of these seven ideas can add significant wealth to your relationship. Which of these seven ideas, and the Treasure Chest book idea in the first chapter, will be your starting point?

1) Explore the treasure of positive intentions
2) Discover the treasure of positive words

3) Distribute the treasure of positive emotions
4) Share the treasure of positive touch
5) Cultivate mindfulness
6) Create positive and valuable time
7) Unearth positive habits

Which of these ideas will you begin your treasure hunt with? You can start stocking your treasure chest with these ideas, and with additional ones on my website. I want to help you find success. Please visit CouplesTreasure.com for additional resources, including ways you can find a therapist in your local area that can help you navigate the terrain of your treasure hunt.

Dr. Richard Nongard, LMFT

Dr. Nongard is the author of numerous books, a frequent conference and keynote speaker, and is available to speak to your organization.

To find out more about how to bring Dr. Richard Nongard as a speaker to your next event, visit

Nongard.com

Please look for other books by Dr. Richard Nongard at your favorite bookseller. Some of his bestselling books include:

The Seven Most Effective Methods of Self-Hypnosis: How to Create Rapid Change in in your Health, Wealth, and Habits

The Step-Spouse: How to Stay Sane When Their Ex is Driving You Crazy

Turn Around Trauma: How to Live Your Best Life After Adversity

Make sure you access the free resources that go with this book.

You can access them now by visiting this website:

CouplesTreasure.com

www.ingramcontent.com/pod-product-compliance
Lightning Source LLC
Chambersburg PA
CBHW031125080526
44587CB00011B/1112